Do You Believe In Miracles?

Angela Lopez
Eugene Sierras

Order this book online at www.trafford.com
or email orders@trafford.com

Most Trafford titles are also available at major online book retailers.

www.trafford.com

North America & international
toll-free: 844 688 6899 (USA & Canada)
fax: 812 355 4082

Our mission is to efficiently provide the world's finest, most comprehensive book publishing service, enabling every author to experience success. To find out how to publish your book, your way, and have it available worldwide, visit us online at www.trafford.com

ISBN: 978-1-6987-1504-9 (sc)
ISBN: 978-1-6987-1505-6 (e)

Library of Congress Control Number: 2023913781

Print information available on the last page.

Trafford rev. 11/29/2023

Casa
de
Inspiración
Arts
Saints
Rosaries
(520)
327-6800
2536 E. 6th St
Tucson, Az
85716

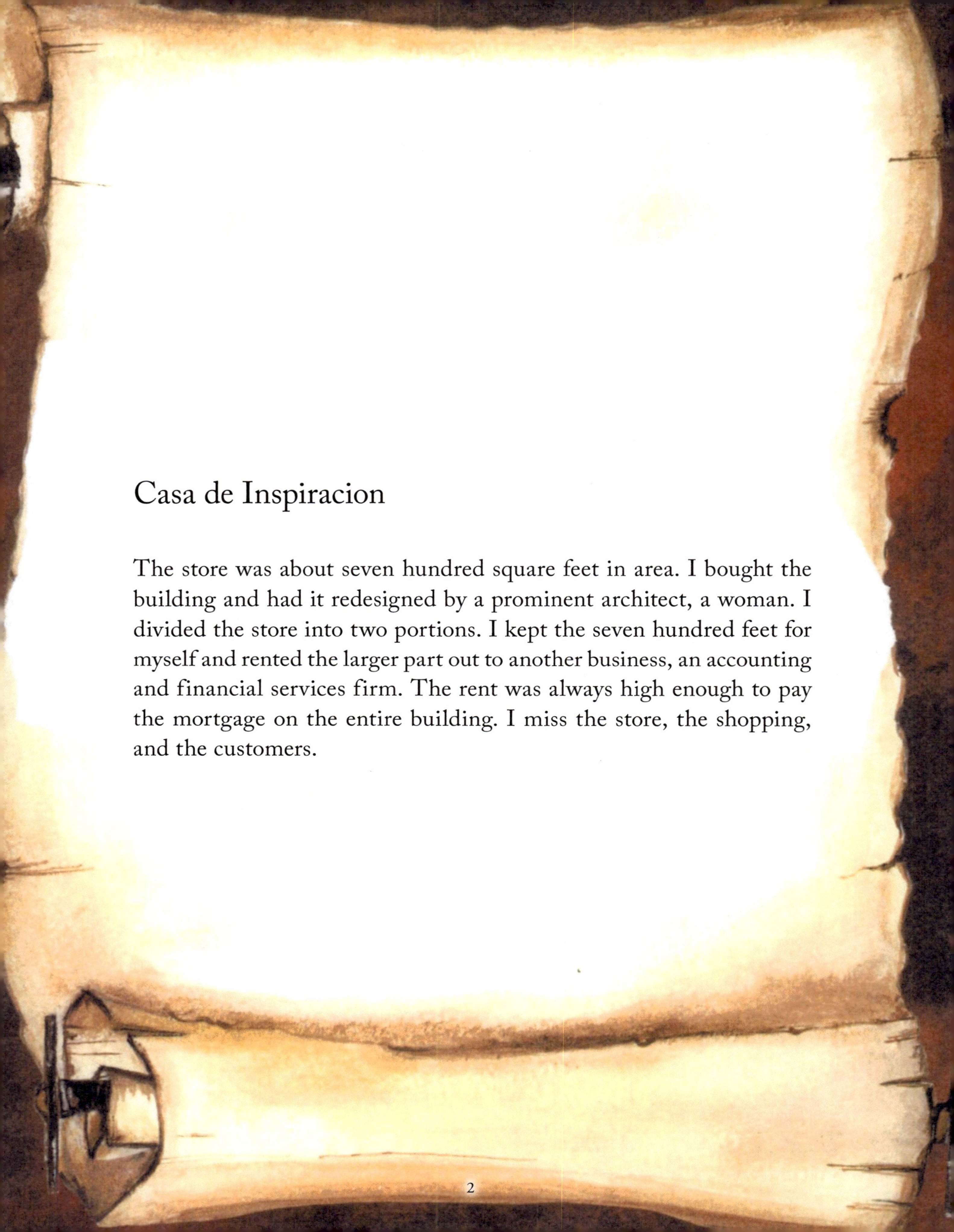

Casa de Inspiracion

The store was about seven hundred square feet in area. I bought the building and had it redesigned by a prominent architect, a woman. I divided the store into two portions. I kept the seven hundred feet for myself and rented the larger part out to another business, an accounting and financial services firm. The rent was always high enough to pay the mortgage on the entire building. I miss the store, the shopping, and the customers.

To Colleen DiBiase, my wonderful friend and business partner, who, without her love for paperwork, this business could not have run as smoothly as it did. We laughed at our difference in shopping and cried at our differences in spending money.

Thank you, also, to Evelyn Valenzuela, my cousin, who had a great part in the success of our inspiring little religious store.

Thank you to all the loyal customers and distributors whose beautiful religious items made this store an exciting venture that Colleen and I can never forget.

Introduction
The inspiration to open a Catholic store began with a dream.

In my dream, God appeared as a kind, old man with a white beard. We conversed. We laughed. After awhile, I asked, "Why are you in my dream?"

"You need to spend more time in prayer," He replied.

Brazenly, I asked, "How much time do You want?"

"Thirty minutes." He replied.

"Just thirty minutes! That does not seem like much to ask. Besides, I already pray for that long or longer." With that last statement we both laughed. I was still laughing when I woke up.

The next day, I timed myself … thirty minutes! I discovered it was, indeed, a long time, twice as long as I normally prayed. I saw that I was not even praying fifteen minutes. I kept getting interrupted by telephone calls, errands, crazy ideas, and distractions. I decided to go pray at the Benedictine convent not far from my house. It provided a quiet, uninterrupted thirty minutes of prayer.

Then I dreamed of God again. As before, we had a pleasant time conversing. Then I asked, "This is the second time you've come to me. Am I going to die?"

"Oh no, you are not ready. You are still getting a D in life!"

"A D in life!" I exclaimed. God was talking to me like the teacher that I was. He said it teasingly, and our laughter, again, woke me up.

That very day, my aunt, Anita, called and asked me for the fourth year in a row to join her on a religious pilgrimage. This time to Betania, Venezuela, where the Virgin Mary had been appearing. Always before, I would refuse. This time I was going to offer this trip to God. I was going on a pilgrimage.

It was during this trip that I was introduced to Saint Anthony. I had a history of always losing or misplacing things, and it was no different on this trip. Cora, Anita's sister, who saw that I was way too often delaying our excursions because I was either looking for my glasses or my purse or something, said, "You need a direct line to Saint Anthony!"

"Saint Anthony! I don't know Saint Anthony. Who is he, and what does he do?" I asked. All saints are known for doing or helping humans in some way. I was not much of a devotee of saints, not like my mother was. I always felt it was better to go to the top.

"He finds things for you, and you need him desperately," Cora replied.

Since this was a religious pilgrimage, we were not only going to Mass and praying fifteen decades of the rosary every day, we were also visiting many religious sites and stores. "OK," I said to Cora, "on our visits to religious stores, when you see a statue of Saint Anthony, show it to me. I'd like to know what he looks like. I'll buy one."

Like clockwork, the very next day and for several days afterward, we were bombarded by Saint Anthony. We went to a church dedicated to Saint Anthony. Then on July 13, we celebrated Saint Anthony's saints day. On the third day, as we were walking by the river where the Virgin appeared, I heard Cora yell at me as she held up some statue. "Angie, here is Saint Anthony!" She was about two blocks away. I went over. I bought the statue. Father Richard, our spiritual director, blessed it using the water of the stream where the Virgin Mary had been appearing. Father Richard was a very devout and pious priest. He had visited the site of the Virgin's appearance several times! The first time, he experienced a miracle. He had cancer of the eye, and it had been cured.

Back at home, as I unpacked, I placed the statue of Saint Anthony on the chest of drawers in my closet. I frivolously spoke to Saint Anthony as if he could hear me. "OK, so you find things." I was a little cocky. "I'll make it easy for you. I bought it several months ago, and I can't find it. Would you please find it for me?" That's all I said. Expecting nothing, I continued unpacking. While standing in front of the statue, I reached up to store a shirt on the top shelf. Suddenly, something fell on the very top of my head! Lo and behold! It was the gold chain I had been looking for. Shocked and very surprised, I spoke to the statue, as if Saint Anthony could hear me. "Did you do this?"

The next day, I met my friend, Colleen, for breakfast. She had just returned from a long trip to Italy. She had several gifts for me. Out of her purse came a magnet and a small, framed picture of Saint Anthony. "I can't believe this," I said, very surprised. "Saint Anthony! What possessed you to get me these items?"

She replied, "I was in Padua where he lived. I could not understand why his tongue was on the altar. Apparently, they desiccated it and sent samples to other churches. Being Catholic, I knew that you would understand this weird practice."

"I have no idea!" I said. "That seems gross!"

I went home and looked for my mother's book on saints. I read that many years after Saint Anthony had died, his body was exhumed. They discovered that his tongue was incorrupt. According to Catholic belief, this is a sure sign of being a saint. After he was canonized, this became a relic. The tongue was desiccated and portions of it were sent as relics to different churches.

That same night I decided to recite the prayer that Colleen had brought back from Padua. I asked for another favor. "OK, I'm going to make it harder for you. Let's see if you can find the medal I bought in Greece two years ago. I've lost it. I have cleaned out all my closets, all my drawers and cannot find it. Guide me." I simply turned around. There in front of me were several shoeboxes. I moved one shoebox out of the way and discovered that behind it was another box. I opened the second box, and there was a third box inside. I opened that box, and there was the medal!

"Wow!" This could not be a coincidence! "Did you guide me?" Again, now it was becoming a habit, speaking to Saint Anthony as if he could answer me.

I immediately called my aunt Anita. "Anita, you won't believe this! But I found the chain and the medal I lost two years ago, all because I asked Saint Anthony!"

Anita, very nonchalant but happy for me, replied, "I'm not surprised!" And she truly was not surprised! For she believed in him and the power of prayer. But I was very surprised!

From that day on, there was a change in how I perceived saints and sacramentals, like religious medals and statues and such.

I remembered that when my dad died, he had pinned on his shirt several medals. I decided that in his honor, I would have one of those medals mounted on a chain. I chose Saint Francis.

The very next day, I took it to a jewelry store. I was wearing the newfound Greek medal and chain. The woman proprietor greeted me and said, "Oh, what a beautiful medal you're wearing."

I replied, "Yes, Saint Anthony recently found it for me. It had been lost."

"That's strange," she said. "We were just talking about Saint Anthony and the miracles he so often performs."

The woman behind the jewelry counter interrupted and said, "I am Jewish. I don't know about Saint Anthony, but I do know about Saint Joseph. A statue of Saint Joseph moves around with me whenever I move. He performed a wondrous miracle for me."

"What kind of miracle?" I asked. I didn't know about Saint Joseph either.

The lady behind the counter became animated. "I lived on the East Coast. I had a house for sale for months and months and months. Someone told me that if I buried a statue of Saint Joseph, I would be able to sell the house pretty fast. I was desperate, so I took her advice. I bought a statue. I went to the part of the house facing the street. And, against my better judgment, I buried the statue as instructed. It is hard for a nonbeliever to believe this, but the very next day, I got not just one offer but three offers. In my opinion, it was an absolute miracle."

"I'm trying to sell two houses. I'm going to leave here, and I am going to buy two statues of Saint Joseph." While I was there, I had them mount Saint Francis of Assisi on a medal.

I immediately drove to Saint Mary's Hospital gift shop. There, I bought two miniature statues of Saint Joseph. I took them to Saint Margaret's Church and knocked on the rectory door. A priest answered. He saw what I was holding and said, "You're not doing with these statues what I think you're doing, are you?"

"Yes, Father," I said.

"I don't believe in that," he replied.

"That's OK, Father. Would you bless them anyway?" He did.

I didn't know at that time that the statues really didn't have to be blessed. It is the prayers and confidence that count. I took them to Anita Street in Barrio Anita and dug a hole to bury one of the statues in front of a house that I had just gutted and refurbished.

As I was stamping down the dirt, a woman standing behind me asked, "Are you selling your house?"

"Yes. Did you see what I just did?" I asked. I had not yet put up any for sale signs. Therefore, I assumed she saw what I had just buried and recognized the significance.

"No!" she replied. "But I'm very interested in buying your house. I've seen you fixing it up, and I want to turn it into a bed-and-breakfast."

I told her the price. "I'll buy it," she said. She bought the house … in cash!

Excitedly, and reassured that Saint Joseph was truly on my side, I went and buried the second statue at the Jerrie Street house. That house took a little longer to sell—a month. But I was nonetheless impressed.

You're supposed to remove the statue and place it in a position of honor in your home. I forgot to do this. But I did buy a large cement statue of Saint Joseph. For a position of honor, I placed him by the front wrought iron gate of my house.

This was the beginning of my interest in saints. This was around 1997.

Another Dream

In 1999, I again had a dream about God. The dream was a happy, cheerful one. We talked. He told me He had an idea. "Open up a Catholic store," He said.

I was teacher. I didn't know anything about a store. "Open a what? A store?" I was surprised.

He replied, "Show people beautiful rosaries, scapulars, and religious statues." I woke up! Thoughts went through my head. That did seem exciting. But I knew nothing about running a store!

In the morning, I remembered the dream and the conversation. I wondered if God really wanted me to open a Catholic store. Many thoughts and questions ran through my head as I got ready for school. I had no idea where a person that owned a store would shop for their inventory, much less rosaries, religious statues, and scapulars!

As usual, the minute I got to school I forgot all about my conversations with God. Working with kids consumes all your energy and thoughts. It wasn't until I was driving home that I tried finding a solution for purchasing religious inventory. I figured I would go to the one store I remembered that was across from St. Augustine Cathedral. I looked it up. It was gone! When did it move? It had being there forever!

However, I did find one on the east side of town. I made up my mind to go talk to the owner on my first Saturday off. She was either too busy to talk or was not interested in encouraging competition. "Oh, I buy from all over," she said when asked. "And if I'm lucky, from vendors who present themselves at my store." I didn't have a store, so there was no way vendors would come to me.

The very next day, I received a totally unexpected call from my cousin, Chata, who lives in Mesa. She never called me, so this call was almost providential. I said, "Chata, I had a dream. I'm supposed to open a store selling Catholic religious statues, scapulars, and rosaries. But it is crazy because I have no idea how nor where to find these wholesale items."

Chata is very religious. She replied, "There's a beautiful store here in Mesa. Come to Mesa." She gave me the name of the store, the name of the woman who ran it, and the location. She told me the woman, Marie, was very kind and would be very helpful.

The following weekend I drove from Tucson to this Catholic store in the Phoenix area. It was a very beautiful, very big store. It even had a chapel in the back. Marie truly was most helpful. "There is a Catholic Marketing Network (CMN) trade show once a year, like the Tucson Gem, Mineral, and Fossil Showcase. They sell all kinds of Catholic merchandise but only to retailors. Vendors from all over the world come. There you will find everything you need for your store," she said.

Colleen, who would soon be retiring from counseling at the same school where I taught, "Do you want to be a partner in a business venture?" I asked.

Every year for I don't know how many years, we would go to the gem show in Tucson. We talked (more liked joked) about how fascinating it would be to have a jewelry store. Well, now was the chance! We would have a fun project! Could I convince her to be my partner? "Do you want to be a partner in running a religious store?" I asked.

"No way! Absolutely not!" She was adamant.

I have no idea how I finally got her to agree. We went on a shopping trip to the CMN convention in Boston. They had just suffered the biggest snowstorm they had had in years. But that didn't stop us. We had fun.

We always laughed a lot. We made silly mistakes, and sometimes I accused her of being funny like Lucille Ball. "No," she said, "I am like Ethel Mertz. You get me into weird situations like the ones that Lucy created for poor Ethel."

We spent $18,000.00 that week at the show. They had beautiful religious items from all over the world. It was difficult not to buy more. Colleen is very cautious. Eighteen thousand drove her crazy. She was horrified! I kept reassuring her that it was necessary that we spend. "You can't have a store if you don't have merchandize." I had to keep repeating myself! "We will survive."

"No one spends that much when starting," she said. Then we ran into Marie from Mesa.

"How much did you spend?" we asked at the same time.

Marie startled Colleen, and we laughed at ourselves, when she graciously answered, "$120,000.00."

As soon as we got home, I started looking for a building suitable for a Catholic store. I never have liked the idea of renting.

"We cannot afford to be at the mercy of a landlord. We need our own building if we are to succeed," I advised Colleen.

I searched all over. I bid on two buildings, but to no avail. Then one day as I was walking home from Rincon Market on Sixth Street near Tucson Boulevard, I saw what I thought was the perfect building. It had just gone up for sale, and it was two blocks away from my house. I called the listing real estate agent, Gary, and exclaimed, "I want to buy the building you have listed across from Rincon Market."

He asked me if I had seen the inside and if I knew how much it was. I replied, "No, how much is it?" We made an appointment for that afternoon. I was afraid someone else would buy it. While there, another person came to look at it. Gary said I was foolish to have told the onlooker that I was buying the building. "Why?" I asked.

"He, obviously, is also interested in buying, and he will outbid you."

Gary was right. But I was determined. That location was perfect for me! I bid $9,000.00 over the asking price and got it. Gary was impressed. He said the man bid $5,000.00 more than the listed price and was certain he would get the building. Gary thought I was smart!

Next, I called an architectural designer whose home I had seen that same year on a home tour. I loved her style. She came and looked at the building and accepted my ideas. She created a beautiful design. It had the flavor of the southwest.

In June of 2000, at our grand opening, Monseigneur Carrillo gave the opening blessing. We were a real store!

Religious Store Customers

The store had an atmosphere that invited conversation. A pretty, antique armchair close to the desk, colorful flowers, green plants, and an oriental rug over the two thousand-year-old shale tile from India. Price tags were placed in a way so they didn't take away from the sanctity of the religious statues.

People would come in and sit in the armchair for a lengthy amount of time. If there were no other customers, they would share, gladly speaking about some religious and beautiful experience. One such woman, an artist who gave us some of her religious tiles to sell on consignment, shared a very memorable incident.

Her family had lost a very important document that they looked for not for days but weeks. They could not find it! The deadline to submit it approached. Together, they sat in a circle and began to pray to the Virgin de Guadalupe. "Please, please help us find this very critical paper, please." Suddenly, there was a loud crash in the room. Saint Anthony's picture that hung on the wall fell to the floor and landed behind a large armoire. "Oh my gosh!" someone said. "We always pray to Saint Anthony. He has always helped us find things! We never asked him. We ignored him. He must be mad at us!" They struggled to move the huge chest. On the floor under the armoire next to the fallen picture of Saint Anthony lay the lost document, all dusty and full of lint!

This was a miracle!

Wooden Angels

An older woman was admitted to a Tucson hospital. She was very sick. She was dying. The doctors announced to her and her husband that there was nothing they could do to save her. They gave her absolutely no hope and very little time to live. Despondent, she tossed in her bed. She thought she had fallen asleep when an angel appeared to her. She said the angel was huge. She, the angel, dominated the whole room. *I've died*, she thought. But then the angel spoke. "You are not going to die. You will live, but you need to do something for me. You need to help others who are in your shoes, who are afraid to be in a hospital or to die."

The apparition (angel) gave her very specific directions as to how to make little—about six-inch tall—wooden angels. These angels were to be shaped in such a way that they would fit into one's hand and remain there even if one fell asleep. They were to be gifted in a little mesh bag with a pretty little prayer. They were meant to take away any fears and negative thoughts about going into surgery or treatment. They were to create confidence in the power of prayer.

"OK, I will do it," the woman answered, now wide awake and self-assured, "if I live."

Again, the apparition said, "Have confidence. You are going to live."

At that moment, several doctors walked into her room. "Somewhat of a miracle has happened! We don't understand it, but your tests are no longer positive. It looks like you are going to be all right. You can go home." They released her.

This confirmed that she had truly seen an angel. She and her husband immediately started on their new project—making beautiful but simple handheld angels. They asked if I would carry them in the store. They became a great success. Somehow, people heard about them. I could hardly keep them in stock.

Angels are the guardians of hope
and wonder, the keepers of magic
and dreams. Wherever there is love,
an angel is flying by.

Your guardian angel knows you
inside and out and loves you just the
way you are. Angels keep it simple
and always travel light.

Remember to leave space in your
relationships so the angels have room
to play. Your guardian angel helps
you find a place when you feel there
is no place to go.

Whenever you feel lonely, a
special angel drops in for tea.

Angels are with you every step of the way and help you soar with
amazing grace.

After all, we are angels in
training, and all we are to do is
spread our wings and fly.

A Photograph of an Angel

A man came in looking for an image of an angel. He didn't know exactly which image, Saint Michael, Saint Gabriel, or Saint Raphael. We showed him what we had: seven archangels, plus the guardian angel. He couldn't decide. People often did that. We, as cradle Catholics, knew angels but never considered the seven different archangels. We knew the Virgin Mary but not the numerous images and names of the apparitions.

Even though we showed him the different images, he couldn't decide. He said that while on vacation he had stopped in front of an ancient church in Europe that was being repaired. It was surrounded by huge scaffolds and construction material. Really, nothing to look at except that it was very, very old. He pulled out his camera and started snapping pictures of what was nothing but uninteresting scaffolds. His wife was curious as to why the sudden interest in an uninteresting subject. He could not explain, so he stopped.

Much later when the negatives were being developed, they were shocked to see a ghostly image of an angel on or in front of the scaffolds. The scaffolds were no less than ten feet tall. The angel was equally as tall. That picture became his favorite of the whole trip. He didn't know what it meant, but he felt he was blessed by it all. He wanted to be reminded of it with an image of an angel in his home.

He asked if he could show me the picture. He carried one in his car.

Distinctly, I was excited to see a transparent image of an angel in front of a very tall building, an old church, with the scaffolds in front.

We could not duplicate the image in the picture in the form of a statue, so he chose to take Saint Michael.

Santo Niño de Atocha

Spirits
Some stories were a bit frightening to me.

Customers sometimes, more often than one would expect, came in asking for religious items in order to rid themselves of "evil" spirits or scary events in their home.

I would help them as much as I could, recommending prayers and medals of Saint Benedictine, novenas to Saint Michael, and so on. I also recommended a particular priest at a particular church in Tucson who knew much more about this type of thing and who could perform exorcism rites if necessary. I did not know at the time that a priest with this title is not supposed to be a public figure to just anyone. He got concerned! Finally, after numerous calls from some of my clients, he asked one woman, "Who has sent you to me?" Needless to say, I think he was a little upset.

Later, I learned that not all apparitions are evil. Spirits appear wanting or needing prayers.

The priest never came to the store, so I'm not sure if anyone told him that I, unknowingly, was the one breaking the church's rules by sending people to him.

I did learn several things from working in the store, however, that helped alleviate some negative occurrences in homes. Sacred salt and holy water are very instrumental in clearing bad energy in a house.

I was fortunate to become acquainted with very traditional priests who would bless salt for us. I ended up collecting a large container of blessed salt and holy water. I would offer these to people who asked for help.

One ex-student of mine came and told me that there was a scary spirit in her house. She had a younger sister, a little girl, a baby. She would stand in her crib, cry, and point at something in the corner of the room. Sometimes the door to her room would get locked from the inside. The family would have to struggle to unlock the door. Always, once the family successfully unlocked the door, the baby girl would be crying and pointing to something in the corner of the room. The family investigated the history of their house. A neighbor revealed that the previous owner, an older woman, had died in that particular room.

They believed that perhaps the older woman's spirit was still lingering there. I gave my ex-student blessed salt and holy water with instructions to sprinkle them in the corners of the room and the entire house as they prayed. Later, she told me that after sprinkling the salt and holy water in all the corners of the house, the baby no longer cried, pointing at some unknown thing in her room. The door no longer got mysteriously locked. The scary and unexplained events stopped.

Santo Niño de Atocha

Santo Nino de Atocha I did not know it then but Santo Nino de Atocha is known to help lost children.

When my uncle Ralph was about four years old he got lost while playing outside, around the corrals at the family ranch. Family and neighbor ranchers spent hours into the early evening looking all over the ranch, which was located in the desert of Avra Valley. They were frantic.

Little Rafael, of course, did not know he was lost. He had been playing with another little boy he met in the arroyo a distance away. When evening started to set in, the little boy started walking Rafael home and left him there to allow Rafael to enter into the corral where some family members were waiting. They were elated to see him, so he didn't understand why he got the scolding of his life. He couldn't understand why they gave him a swat in the rear after acting so happy he had finally returned.

"?Donde has estado todas estas horas? Te hemos buscado por dondequiera!!!" (Where have you been all these hours? We have looked all over for you!)

"I was playing with a little boy, and he even walked me back to the ranch." He told them that he had been jumping over rocks in the arroyo when he met this little boy. They jumped over rocks all the way home.

"What little boy? There are no little boys for miles around here," they asked. He pointed to a picture on the wall and told them it was that little boy. The picture on the wall was that of Santo Nino de Atocha.

Santo Nino de Atocha is a Roman Catholic image of the Christ child popular among the Hispanic cultures of Spain and the southwestern United States. He is distinctly characterized by a staff and a drinking gourd (used to carry water) and a basket of bread that he served to prisoners who were thirsty and hungry in the prisons of Spain. He wears a cape, which is fixed to a scallop shell, a symbol of a pilgrimage to Saint James.

The family talked about this incident for years. My uncle Ralph, as he grew, became very devout to Santo Nino de Atocha. When he died, as a memorial, I gave the family a cement statue of Santo Nino de Atocha from the store.

A Big, Black Dog to the Rescue

Sister Ramona was accustomed to walking early in the morning and late in the evening just before dusk. One evening as she was strolling just before dusk, she noticed a car slowly following her. In the car were several "hoodlum" looking young men. They began to harass her. The car pulled up next to her and slowly kept pace with her. They appeared to realize that she was a nun and begun to make unkind remarks. She became frightened. Suddenly, a huge, black dog came up to her and gingerly walked alongside her, between her and the car. The dog growled at the men harassing her. However, his vicious noises must have scared them. They sped off and left her alone. The dog walked her back to the monastery. Then it disappeared into the night. She doesn't know where that dog came from or where it went. She says that she earnestly believes that it had to have been an angel. She knew that the dog meant to threaten the men and scare them off. She was thankful.

A Little Girl Dressed in White
Sister Carmela told me a story about a nun.

One of the nuns at the monastery in Clyde, Missouri, suffered from dementia or maybe early Alzheimer's. One day, she left the monastery and went for a walk. She walked into the forest surrounding the monastery. Then she could not find her way back and began to cry. Suddenly, she saw a little girl in a white dress. The little girl approached her and asked, "Why are you crying?"

"I'm lost!" the nun sobbed.

The little girl said, "Don't cry. I'll take you back home. Don't cry!"

She took the elderly lady by the hand and led her back to the monastery and rang the doorbell. To this day, they don't know who that little girl was. The nuns believed that it had to have been an angel. They had never seen that little girl before, and they have never seen her again.

Who was she? Was she an angel?

A Nurse Dressed in White Wearing an Old Fashioned Cap

My brother, Raul Lopez, was a patient at the university hospital. He had leukemia and was undergoing rigorous experimental chemotherapy treatments. Most of the day, Charlene, his wife, would stay with him. However, at night she would leave. One night, he had a very unusual experience. He desperately had to go to the restroom. He pressed the nurse call button, but no one responded. He forced himself out of bed and then had a horrible, embarrassing, and messy accident. He thought, *This is dreadful! How humiliating! The hospital will hate me when they are forced to clean this up.*

It was even more embarrassing when a beautiful, young nurse dressed in white and wearing a little cap came to assist him. "I am so very sorry," he said, totally humiliated.

"That's OK, Raul. Don't worry, I'll clean it up." She reassuringly repeated, "Don't worry. Accidents always happen in the hospital." She sat him down, found a clean gown, helped him clean up, and finally put him to the bed.

After she left, a second nurse came into the room and apologized to him. "I am so sorry I took so long to respond. I am the only nurse in this section tonight. How can I help you?"

He responded, "No, I don't need any more help. The other nurse already came in and helped."

The second nurse said, "There is no other nurse here. Unfortunately, I am the only one tonight."

"The one dressed in white with a little white cap, you know, like nurses used to wear. She came in and helped me," he said.

"There is no one like that here. 1am the only one tonight," she repeated.

Raul was insistent. "No, someone came in and helped me."

He later said to me, "That had to have been an angel. I was so embarrassed and didn't want to face a hospital worker knowing the mess I had made. God must have felt sorry for me."

He was very religious. Actually, I should say he was very spiritual. He swore that it had to have been an angel that spared him the horrible humiliation of facing the real hospital workers.

Saint Anthony Finds the Love of Your Life Not only does he find lost articles but he also finds the love of your life.

I had a stubborn, old friend, Richard, who had stage-four cancer. As he got weaker, his childhood and college friend, Gene, and I helped him take care of some of his daily chores. We, along with other friends, also took turns taking him to his doctors. But as bad off as he was, he insisted on being as independent as possible. He worried that he was infringing on his friends' personal lives.

For example, Gene's wife had passed away the year previous. Richard insisted that he was lonely and that he needed to meet a woman he could talk to, with whom he could go to dinners, movies, and so on. He wanted me to introduce Gene to some of my single friends. That, in my opinion, was a big responsibility. I didn't know Gene too well. Even though we had both been in the same Catholic school in first and second grade, we didn't meet again until after his college years. It took time before I consented to introduce him to some of my friends; after all, Gene seemed to be a very intelligent and considerate person.

I arranged for him to meet three or four different friends. It never worked out. I finally decided he needed more help than I could offer. I introduced him to Saint Anthony. I gave him a little statue and told him to put it face down. "Ask Saint Anthony to send to you the love of your life. Say prayers to him."

We started going out to lectures and plays. I asked him to sit alone so that it didn't look like he had a mate. "And talk to the single women."

Finally, one day, he cornered me. "I have to give Saint Anthony back to you."

I asked, "Why? Have you given up? Or did you find someone?"

He replied, "No, I am not giving up. I think I found the love of my life."

"Oh no! I'm jealous! We aren't going to be able to do things together anymore. Do I know her?"

“Very well!” he replied.

“Really? Who is she?”

“You.” He smiled sheepishly.

“Oh no! I don’t want a relationship. I don’t need a partner!” I handed back the Saint Anthony statue.

“It’s OK,” he said kindly. “I can wait or we can go along as we are.”

Later, I rehashed the scenario and felt it was too silly of me not to give this opportunity a chance. After all, I really liked and respected him. He was a good Catholic. He was very intelligent. And he was a very caring and helpful friend. He had also stood by his sick wife for ten years, caring and helping her. He had high morals. And I loved conversing and spending time with him.

I decided to give this adventure a chance. And, not surprisingly, we did fall in love. We ended up getting married a year later.

Saint Anthony as Matchmaker

A woman came into the store with a friend, who had been advised that if she wanted to meet the love of her life, she needed to have a statue of Saint Anthony.

We laughed and assured her that we had seen this relationship with Saint Anthony work and people had found the love of their lives.

The statue that we had in the store at the time was from Mexico. Saint Anthony carried a removable Baby Jesus in his arms. In Mexico, they made a request, they prayed, and they believed in taking the Baby Jesus away from Saint Anthony. They returned Baby Jesus to Saint Anthony's arms when the request was granted. That seemed rather unpleasant. The way I rationalized this is that seeing Saint Anthony without Jesus was a reminder to pray.

The customer took the statue. She decided to put the statue face down instead of taking Jesus from his arms. That same evening, her little dog became very ill. She called the veterinarian clinic, but they were closed. She had a friend whose brother was a retired veterinarian. She called and begged him to take a look at her little dog. Up to that time, they had never met, but when they met, something clicked for both of them. She called me the next day. She asked, "Can Saint Anthony work that fast? Am I overreacting? I met someone that I really like."

To make a long story short, they ended up falling in love and getting married. By the way, her dog recovered, and she attributed it all to Saint Anthony.

Another Lost Item for Saint Anthony

A woman lost her diamond earring. She had to have lost it in or around her house, as she knew she was wearing it all day at home. It had much sentimental value besides being quite expensive.

She looked everywhere she could think of, traced every step she took that day, but it was useless, she told me. She couldn't find it no matter how carefully she inched through the house and yard. Before giving up, she said a prayer to Saint Anthony. Then she went to bed.

The next morning as she went for a walk, she saw something shining right next to the sidewalk. Totally astounded, she saw that it was her diamond earring. She found it in the very spot where she had looked the day before. "There it was!" she said to her friend. "I walked that spot thousands of times yesterday, searching and searching. I know I would have seen it if it had been there." She was sure Saint Anthony found it for her.

The Virgin de Guadalupe

One day, an author came into the store and asked if we would carry her book on consignment. Her name was Lourdes Walsh. (I learned later that the name she wrote under was C. Lourdes Walsh.)[1] The name of the book was *The Story of Our Lady of Guadalupe, Empress of the Americas*.[2] It was a beautiful book with incredibly colorful illustrations explaining the story behind the vision of Our Lady of Guadalupe.

This book taught me many new and miraculous details about her apparition. Below I list some of the details I found astounding.

"In 1929 the official photographer of the old Basilica of Guadalupe discovered the image of a man in one of the Virgin's eyes. He reported his finding to ophthalmologist, Dr. Rafael Torrija Lavoignet, who, in great detail, examined the eyes of the Virgin's image with an ophthalmoscope.. He observed a very apparent human figure in the corneas of both eyes, with the location and same distortion occurring naturally in a human eye.

1. "In 1979, using digitized high resolution images, magnified 2,500 times, Dr. Jose Aste Tonsmann discovered that in addition to the human bust others had previously seen, other human figures were reflected in the Virgin's eyes: a total of thirteen people. The same people are present in both the left and right eyes, in different proportions, a natural occurrence when human eyes reflect the objects that are before them. He believes the reflection transmitted by the eyes of the Virgin of Guadalupe is the scene on December 9, 1531, during which Juan Diego showed his tilma to Bishop Juan de Zumarraga and others.
2. "Nuclear physicist, Dr. Charles Wahlig, also posited that the Blessed Mother must have been invisibly present when Juan Diego presented the roses to Bishop Zumarraga. The tilma acted as a photographic plate that captured her image, and the reflection of their images in her eyes."[3]

---

[1] C. Lourdes Walsh, originally from New York City, is a former Catholic nun who served a number of years among the poor in Mexico.

[2] C. Lourdes Walsh, *The Story of Our Lady of Guadalupe Empress of the Americas* (Sarasota, Florida: Arcade Lithographers, 1948).

[3] "Our Lady of Guadalupe: The Holy Virgin's Miraculous Self-Portrait," Monastery Icons, Windows into Heaven, https://www.monasteryicons.com/product/The-Holy-Virgins-Miraculous-Self-Portrait/.

3. The flowers on her robe were flowers blooming in the area during the month of December on top of Tepeyac. Ironically, Tepeyac Hill had previously been the location of an Aztec temple to a pagan goddess, Tonantzin, the Snake Woman. The Aztecs considered Tonantzin, Coatlicue, Cihuacéatl, or Tetéoinan as "the divine mother," a protector of women.[4]
4. The roses that filled Juan Diego's tilma were Castilian roses, which grew only in Spain.
5. The name Guadalupe was also the name of a river in Spain whose source is near a small village of the same name found in the region of Extremadura, near the Portuguese border. It is also believed that the word comes from a corruption of a word in the native language Nahuatl.
6. The stars on Our Lady of Guadalupe's cloak are in the exact position of the constellations as seen on December 12, 1531, when Juan Diego encountered her.[5]
7. The black ribbon around Mary's waist shows that she is expecting a child. That was what an expectant Aztec princess would wear.
8. The Virgin stands on a crescent moon. The Aztec word for Mexico, "Metz-xic-co", means "in the center of the moon." The moon also symbolized the Aztec moon god, fertility, birth and life.[6] Juan Diego's tilma was made from the fiber of the agave plant. This plant is native to Mexico as well as other regions in South America and is used not only for clothing but also for medicinal purposes and, specifically blue agave, is used in the production of tequila.

Juan Diego's tilma has lasted for five hundred years and has maintained its chemical and structural integrity. Most replicas of tilmas made with the same chemical and structural composition last only about fifteen years! In addition, the tilma was displayed for about 115 years before it was placed in protective glass and was subject to such things as soot, candle wax, incense, and human touch. Scientists are unable to explain why it has lasted so long.[7]

4 https://www.theyucatantimes.com/2020/12/tonantzin-the-deity-behind-our-lady-of-guadalupe/

5 https://www.myguadalupe.com/symbolism.html

6 Ibid.

7 http:/blog.magiscenter.com/blog/the-science-or-lack-thereof-behind-juan-diegos-tilma

"There are several parts of the cloth which have been painted on some time after the original image was created. These parts include the moon underneath the Virgin's feet, the angel holding the cloth, and the rays coming from the image. The original image of the Virgin herself, however, does not appear to have been touched by an artist. There is no sketch underneath it, no brush strokes, and no corrections. It appears to have been produced in a single step. These features were identified through scientific testing conducted by Dr. Philip Serna Callahan, who was a biophysicist at the University of Florida, and a NASA consultant. He photographed the image under infrared light, and published his findings in 1981 in a paper called 'The Tilma under Infrared Radiation.'."[8]

[8] Ibid.

Roses de la Virgin Guadalupe

Lillian, the neighbor lady who lives across the street, who isn't religious, or at least claims not to be, came and knocked on my door one day. "I need you to see something," she said. "I have placed in the backyard a tile with a painting of the Virgin de Guadalupe. It came from a house that belonged to my grandmother. When she died, the house came up for sale. The new owners kindly let me remove it from the wall on the condition that I would fix and plaster the area from where I removed it." It was sentimentally valuable to Lillian not only because it was valued by her grandmother but also because her grandmother had painted the image.

We walked into her yard. "I brought the tile home and placed it right here." She showed me the very large mosaic image sitting on the ground and up against her patio wall. "Look what happened!" She said. "See these two roses here? I didn't plant any roses. These two white roses just grew. They showed up all by themselves."

Yes, there stood two pretty roses in front of the Virgin de Guadalupe.

I didn't have an explanation. I told her that when the Virgin de Guadalupe appeared to Don Diego, she presented him with roses. Roses and the fragrance of roses are significant when it comes to the images and apparitions of the Virgin Mary.

Loss of Faith

Why would a little six-year-old girl who prayed the rosary every night before going to sleep, who always, in spite of often being scolded, left a little of bit of food on her plate for her guardian angel, who grew up guided by prayers and petitions to God, grow up to lose her faith? Always asking God to help her pass a test, to fix a broken statue so her mother wouldn't notice, and even in college, to help her pass the rigorous pre-English exam, why did she lose her faith when it seemed that her prayers were always answered?

For about five years, starting at the age of twenty-six, I lost my faith and belief in God. It was a very difficult surprise to many, especially my aunt Anita, who had guided me along, believing I was very special.

It was a gradual questioning of the religion, which started after my brief university study in Guadalajara and simultaneous tour of Mexico City. As we toured this beautiful metropolis, the guides, who, by the way, worked for a government that was very anti-Catholic, informed us of terrible deeds committed by the Catholic Church, its priests, and its nuns. My disillusionment was reinforced by seeing the suffering of the very indigent, who seemed to be the most faithful and charitable of Catholics.

At the same time, I was reading great books by avowed atheist Ayn Rand.[9] I liked what she said and started thinking like her.

When I returned to the States, I began to dislike the homilies by a fire-and-brimstone, very well-fed, fat monseigneur (anyway, that's how I saw him). *One of these days, I am going to walk out and not come back*, I thought. He scolded and yelled from the pulpit. "You are all sinners! You don't support the church as you should!" (I wonder now if that's what he meant, but that's what I heard, probably because of my attitude.)

Then the final straw! A bomb in one of the Los Angeles International Airport lockers exploded and killed some children. I decided God would not let this happen. Therefore, there must be no God. If God were there, these terrible things would not happen.

---

[9] A Russian-born American writer and philosopher, Rand was born and educated in Russia before she moved to the United States in 1926. She is known for her fiction and for developing a philosophical system named objectivism.

I also learned something about myself. I could be good. I could do good without God and without always fearing the devil. I found that it was still important to me to live by good standards. "Do onto others as you would have them do unto you." "For every action, there is an equal and opposite reaction." "Be the best version of yourself." These and many other fatherly statements ran through my head. I had parents who believed in me. I would not let them down.

Nonetheless, they were very disappointed in me, especially my aunt Anita. Often, she would tell me that she was praying for me. "You know," I said one day, "if there is a God, wouldn't He see me as one of His lost sheep? And wouldn't He find it important to come after me? He hasn't done that. Why? Because He doesn't exist!"

"He will," she said.

"Oh, great! I hope He doesn't make horrible things happen to me, causing me to fall on my knees, begging for help." She laughed but thought I was pompous.

Well, five things did happen. But if I remember correctly, it was after I began to delve into the studies of parapsychology. When I went to some of these sessions, the instructors would make sure that they and the participants pray for protection. In the astral projection session, the leader said, "It is very important that you ask for the protection of angels. That way no evil spirit can overpower you."

"What?" I asked myself. My big relief in not believing in God was that if there is no God, there is no afterlife and there are no spirits. (I grew up believing in and fearing ghosts and the devil.) This was a big challenge now.

I had a very religious, Seventh-day Adventist friend who was very active in her church and its fun activities. She asked me to some of these activities. I felt good going to the services and decided to search out other religions. None were very satisfying.

One day while on a ski trip, my mother called me and said my brother, whom I loved very much, was in the hospital and possibly had intestinal cancer. "Pray," I said to her. "Call all the relatives and ask them to pray. I will come home as soon as I can." I tried to console her. She didn't want me to do that. She didn't want to unnecessarily instill fear in my brother. He still didn't suspect cancer, and my coming home would cause him to see the seriousness of the visit.

Fall on my knees! I did just that. I went to the neighboring church. "Ok, God! Is this one of those times when you are asking me to pray for a miracle?" I prayed and prayed!

My mother prayed, "Don't let this happen to my son. If anyone must suffer cancer, let it be me." The weekend went by, and on Monday, the family, without me, met with the hospital doctor. "Mrs. Lopez," he said to my mother and my brother's wife, "I can't believe this, but the biopsy came in. I have seen cancer. I have smelled cancer. When I operated on your son, I was certain he had cancer. It is a sure miracle. He doesn't have cancer."

My brother was surprised. He did not know that there had been the possibility of cancer. He remained in the hospital for weeks, as he had had a ruptured intestine caused by diverticulitis. After being cured, he gave up drinking and smoking and turned to God big time.

I had four more causes to fall on my knees and pray for a miracle, still not quite sure there was a God, but I guess getting closer and closer to believing.

I don't remember the exact sequence of events but there was a huge fire in the canyon where we lived in California. Firemen were all over the canyon, around the brush, and on our roof fighting the fire. I walked into the house (it was 4 p.m., and I was coming home after teaching all day).

My three stepchildren were in the kitchen stupefied by the fire, each holding a favorite animal, one a dog, the other a hamster, and the third a pet chicken. At my direction, they ran outside and waited at our designated fire emergency stop. I ran down to the bottom floor to turn on the sprinkler system. Foolishly, I thought this would help. As I opened the door to the outside, a fury of flames lapped at my face almost setting my hair on fire. I ran upstairs, met the girls, and ran down the opposite hill to my principal's house as sparks of burning brush fell on our heads and yelping dog.

As my principal drove me back, I kept praying that the house was still there. When we reached there, the fire chief came up to me and asked if I was the owner of the house. He said, "I don't know if you believe in miracles, but it is a miracle your house did not burn down. The wind stopped suddenly, and we were able to control the flames. We did far more damage to your roof than the fire did to your house. It was a miracle." He repeated this several times.

Jena, My Seven-Year-Old Stepdaughter

Jena was another cause for deep prayer and the need for God's help, if He was there.

Julie and Jennifer ran upstairs crying and seeking our help. "Jena is knocked out. She was doing back flips on the wooden A-frame horse, and she hit her head as she came down. She isn't waking up." They were hysterical. We ran downstairs, picked her up, and rushed her to the hospital. She was pretty incoherent and obviously hurt. The doctors assured us that they would do everything they could to find out the extent of what they figured was a concussion. They required that we leave her at the hospital for further examinations and observation.

As early as we were allowed back in the hospital, we called for the doctor. Happily, he came to greet us. "You can take this miraculous little girl home. There is nothing wrong with her. You can count your blessings." Was that another miraculous event? I didn't think about it too much at the time.

This One Was More Dramatic

My mother called me while I was living in California. "You have to come home. Your father will have to have surgery. They think he has a brain tumor."

I rushed buying a plane ticket and went home. My parents were very important to me, and the thought of losing one of them was more than I could stand.

My father went through a series of very serious tests and examinations. He was very religious, and he prayed with much fervor that nothing be wrong. A week or so after the series of exams, the doctors seemed stumped. They couldn't figure why the symptoms did not match their previous diagnosis. They threw their hands up in the air. It was not a tumor. They did not have to operate. We were elated.

My dad took these results very seriously. This was no coincidence and no accident. It had to be an answer to prayer. He felt he needed to make a pilgrimage of gratitude to God. He decided to make a pilgrimage to the mission in Magdalena, Mexico. Hispanics often made pilgrimages to Father Kino's mission where Saint Xavier's relics lie. This was done as a sign gratitude or as a petition for help. Some people walked the distance as penance. We drove. It is a long ride of about 110 miles across the border and through the desert.

While there, I am embarrassed to say that my mother and I did some shopping instead of joining my father in prayer and teased that he was so "superstitious."

We left Magdalena. My dad felt satisfied that he had shown to God his sincere gratitude. When we arrived home, my father and mother immediately went grocery shopping. I decided to vacuum. As I was putting the vacuum cleaner away, I experienced an electrical shock go through my head and down my lower back. I made it to the couch, and as soon as I lay down, the pain disappeared. *What a strange phenomenon*, I thought. But no sooner than I got up, the incredible pain reappeared. When my parents came home, I could hardly explain what was happening.

My mother was insistent that it was all in my head. She couldn't figure why if I lay in bed, there was no pain but if I even just sat up, the pain was excruciating. This went on for weeks. If I went to the table, I had to eat with my head parallel to the floor.

Because I was from out of town, getting to see a doctor took weeks. When I was finally able to secure an appointment, I endured a lengthy series of X-rays and exams! Most were done while sitting or standing. Sinus infection and migraines were ruled out.

Finally, on the sixth week, because neurologists were so booked up, they indicated that the only way they could see me was to go through the emergency ward. My mother drove me to the hospital. I lay prone in the back seat. This time I prayed that if there was a God, He let me die.

In the doctor's office at the hospital, I sat, again with my head parallel to the floor. "What you are describing," the doctor said, "could be very serious. Either you are a neurotic, or five very dangerous things could occur if not corrected." He enumerated the five things. I think he was trying to scare me into admitting that I had nothing wrong. "You could end up paralyzed with a stroke, you could lose your sense of speech, you could go blind, you could end up retarded, you could lose your eye sight, or, worse, you could die."

"I am not neurotic," I replied.

"In that case, let's find out what is wrong," he said. "We will do a spinal tap." They wheeled me into the dressing room and then into the waiting room.

As I sat there, an older woman, a patient, sat near me. We talked, "I am waiting to have a spinal tap," I said when she asked.

"You poor dear! They use a needle this long to go into your spine." She stretched her hands about six inches. (Today, I suspiciously wonder if she wasn't sent out to scare me into admitting to my "phony pain.")

When on the examination table, I asked the doctor if they were using a huge needle. He laughed and showed me the tiny needle that, supposedly, he was using.

"Well, by golly!" he finally declared. "Sure enough, you have blood in your spinal fluid. The good thing is that it looks old and not fresh." They admitted me into the hospital under very strict orders not to sit up or get up. I was there a week. I had all kinds of tests. Nothing was giving them the information that they needed to diagnose the problem. Finally, an angiogram was ordered. I had to sign release papers stating that it was a dangerous procedure and that I could possibly die if a tumor was blocking the arteries. It didn't scare me, but I felt anguish for my mother, who had been losing a different member of her immediate family every two years for the last twelve years. I asked the doctor not to say anything to anyone in the family.

The results came in. They were never able to diagnose why I had headaches nor the source of the blood. In the process, however, they found that I had a very small aneurism, not dangerous, but one that had to be watched and examined every five years. They enumerated some limitations: no skydiving, no deep-sea diving, and no lifting of more than fifty pounds.

"Go home to California. You are going to be all right. You are a lucky girl," the nurses reassured me.

While in California, I ended up having another angiogram. The headaches returned after getting on a roller coaster at Magic Mountain. The result was the same. No conclusion. But the headaches finally diminished. Was God giving me a message?

I Had a Dream

I dreamed my mother was dying. It was recurring. I felt guilty because it had been my father who had been ill, not my mother. Was I being selective? Finally, the dream was so real, I decided I had to move back to Tucson, not that I thought it was a premonition but a facing-up to the fact that my parents needed me and someday, they might die and I emotionally needed to be home.

When I awakened, I was determined to put up for sale the house I had just purchased just two years earlier. I loved the house but had to sell it and return home. I remember going to the nursery and buying blooming flowers. My neighbor peeked over the fence. "What are you doing?" she asked.

"These flowers are going to sell my house." I replied, and she laughed.

Two weeks later, the house sold. I called a moving company, packed my things, and moved to Tucson. But before I moved, I went and spent two days with a very special friend and her husband. One night, we went to a psychic fair and had several readings. I didn't like what I heard. "Be very careful with whom you mix company. There is a mafia man who will find you very attractive. You are very intuitive. Intuition comes in your dreams." The latter was the worst thing I could hear. I was moving to Tucson because of a dream. I didn't want to be intuitive!

What frightened me most was that my mother was ill. Two months after I arrived in Tucson, she was diagnosed with breast cancer. She died the following year.

I stopped dreaming! Or, at least, I stopped remembering my dreams. I was pretty depressed and started walking the canyon every chance I got.

Sundays were the best. My father was wanting to see me go to church. Every Sunday, he would ask, "*Mi hijita*, did you go to church?"

"Yes, Dad. I went to church."

"Where did you go?" It was always the same short dialogue.

"I went to God's Church."

"Where is that?"

"Sabino Canyon."

"Oh!" He would just smile, never showing a negative feeling but always hoping that I would go to a real Sunday Mmass.

Maybe his prayers were answered. I started visiting the Benedictine Monastery, a familiar place to me during my college days. I had found and now continue to find much solitude there, almost like a bucket of love and grace is thrown over me as soon as I walk in. I started going to Mass after my walks at the canyon. Before I knew it, I was hooked. I went not just on Sundays but also during the week to the 5 p.m. Mmass and times in between. No one knew me, so I felt very comfortable walking in to Mass in my hiking clothes. I think that was the beginning of my return to the Catholicism. It felt so good, so natural, so inspiring.

Christmas Time at the Store

I believe customers sometimes waited until Christmas time to buy our most expensive items. During that season, we would give a big Christmas discount on all our merchandise to our regular customers.

Poinsettias, evergreen wreathes, and nativities galore decorated the store. We had antique and new nativities, large and small, and from many parts of the world. We had beautiful nativity scenes that ranged from twenty-six dollars to eight hundred dollars. We tried to make everything look pretty. It didn't look like a store that just sold merchandise. It was supposed to make one feel good. One woman said looking at the displays was the highlight of her Christmas season. What a wonderful compliment!

Selling items at a huge discount during this time really cut into our profits, however. But I had made up my mind that getting beautiful religious items into homes was my real objective. Both my business partner and I were retired from the education system. We got retirement checks, so we didn't have to worry about an income. However, we did work for almost nothing and had our share of worries about staying up with our bills. I must clarify: it was Colleen that had her share of worries. I would do the shopping and spending, and she would deal with the taxes and bills. I was the one who had the fun, she would remind me, or scold me, depending on her mood. We got along beautifully though. It was like Lucy Ricardo and Ethel Mertz. Lots of laughter. Sometimes tears.

We had an exquisite four-foot bronze statue of the Virgin de Guadalupe. It stood in a very prominent spot in the store. It was sculptured by an artist who created a limited number in order to donate his profits to an anti-abortion organization. He was able to sell them for thousands of dollars.

We loved the statue and thought that we would enjoy it for a long time because no one would buy it at the price at which it was listed. Besides, we didn't mind having invested the money that it took for us to buy it. It gave our store class! However, Christmas came and the invitations with the big Christmas discount crushed our dream. Colleen and I cried when the bronze Virgin de Guadalupe statue sold. Our consolation was that it went to one of our best customers, a beautiful woman and her family who had bought many religious items throughout the years.

The Silver Egg Icon

My thrill was to find beautiful and unusual religious items. Any time we traveled, any time the gem show came into town, any time the CMN show back east was holding its gathering, finding beautiful, one-of-a-kind items was exciting. My best buys were things that I personally would have loved to own but for which I no longer had room or sometimes not enough money.

There was one very expensive little icon painted on a ceramic egg, which fit snuggly inside a silver pendant that opened and shut. Icons cannot be signed; however, it was obvious this one was painted by a famous Russian iconographer. A woman, who worked at the university nearby, admired it for almost a year. Often she came in, picked it up, and held it, wishing to buy it. Sadly, she felt it was too expensive for her budget. For that whole year, other people, too, admired that one-inch or so little icon. Evelyn, who was a very caring sales person, tried to encourage clients to layaway anything that they loved but could not buy right at the time. "This is one of a kind. We will not be getting another," she would say. I think sometimes they didn't quite believe that to be true.

I remember the day the woman who worked at the university came in. She excitedly opened the door and exclaimed, "I am taking the little silver egg!" She was very happy. I felt so badly when I told her that it had just sold the day before. She couldn't believe it.

That happened many times with other items as well. It seemed like once someone lay their eyes on something, it attracted other eyes. We would advise our customers that if they liked an item and couldn't yet afford it to place it on layaway. Sometimes we had layaways for six months or so with people making small monthly payments when they could.

The Young Man Who Purchased a Statue for His Mother

A young man placed a beautiful, six-hundred-and-fifty-dollar, four-foot statue of the Virgin Mary on layaway. It was never a problem to keep these large statues on layaway because they dressed up our store with their beauty. He struggled but finally made his final payment just in time to give it to his mother for her birthday. However, there was a problem. His car broke down. "No problem," we said. "We will deliver it." As I drove up to the house, I was struck by how poor they seemed to be. Six hundred and fifty dollars had to have been a lot of money to this family. But the significance of a lovely religious image in their house was more important. They certainly were rich in spirit. It reminded me of a passage in the Bible, Luke 21:1–6.[10]

[10] "As Jesus looked up, he saw the rich putting their gifts into the temple treasury. He also saw a poor widow put in two very small copper coins. 'Truly I tell you,' he said: 'This poor widow has put in more than all the others.'"

My Personal Miracle: The Retablo

A retablo is a small devotional painting usually on tin derived from traditional Catholic art.

When New Mexico was a young and very Catholic Spanish colony, the people, who were isolated, longed to have access to the religious art that they had left behind in their mother country. Retablos became the solution. In Latin American, the people started painting traditional Catholic art forms on tin, if they had tin, or wood if they didn't have the tin.

The idea came to me to do the same thing. I felt very saddened when we started sending troops to bomb Afghanistan, to create a war. I decided to say my prayers through art. I went to the garage, pulled out a 16-inch x 3-foot piece of lumber, gathered my paintbrushes and acrylic paints, and started to paint a retablo. I chose the Virgin de Guadalupe as my subject. I spread out in front of me numerous pictures of her image and as I spoke to her, I painted. Six or seven hours went by and then I remembered my engagement for dinner at my brother's house. I hated to leave my project, but I had reached a stumbling block anyway. I am not an artist, and sketching her face was going to be a challenge. *I will stop here and later call my friend, Annie, who is an outstanding artist, to finish up the face and hands*, I thought. I left to go to dinner.

When I got back home, I had second thoughts. "An art picture is just paint! If I make a mistake, then I can call Annie to repaint the face," I said to myself. I picked up the brush and paints and started painting. Her face turned out beautiful. Her hands were OK. I went to bed pretty satisfied.

In the morning, I painted the angel and cushion at her feet. Then I noticed something unique. The face and neck showed two things I had not painted, nor even thought of painting: the muscle between the nose and the upper lip on the face[11] and the tendon under the neck that shows when one is stressed.[12] Also, if I looked at her face from the side, I could see a streak that created a tear running down from one of her eyes. I didn't know if I had been blessed with a miracle from her or I was just wanting to be special.

I showed it to Sister Carmel and when I spoke to an artist who came to the store, he volunteered to make a saguaro frame for it.

[11] The levator labii superioris alae-que nasi is the muscle that dilates the nostrils and raises the upper lip.

[12] The sternocleidomastoid are muscles on either side of the neck that are contracted when the head rotates to the side, or the chin is titled upward.

Saint Michael the Archangel
Miraculous events sometimes happen in mysterious ways.

Coming home from school, and as I reached my home, a huge Silverado truck racing toward me gave a left turn right in front of me and hit me head on. The driver of the truck ran from her vehicle and apologized profusely, repeating, "I didn't see you. I didn't see you," over and over as she cried.

I remember saying, and later regretting my lack of sympathy, "That was a stupid thing to do!" I was angry that my beloved little Honda looked like it was totaled. (And, indeed, I found out later, it was totaled!)

The fortunate thing (blessed thing) is that I was not hurt. The only damage inside the car was the dislodging of a little metal visor clip of Saint Therese the Little Flower. It had fallen on my lap. In spite of my saying that I was not injured, the paramedics insisted on taking me from the "wrecked car" to the hospital. They would not believe that I was OK. "You could have dislocated a vertebrae, and one wrong move could leave you an invalid." They scared me. I didn't resist, nor did I then move an inch on my own!

Later, after I was released from the hospital, I developed a stiff neck. I could hardly turn my head. The stiffness lingered for days and days, even though I was treated by a chiropractor, until one evening when I was working on my income taxes.

When I remodeled my house, I decided to build an indoor lap pool. I had been told that I had scoliosis and daily swimming would be the best therapy. Going to the gym and waiting for a scheduled swim time was going to be too tedious. I figured, since I had the space, an indoor pool was a great solution. That idea turned out to be a fiasco that I won't even address. The five-foot deep pool remained unfinished for several years. Danger was lurking there. Two of my dogs had fallen in, danger to one only because the shepherd was so big.

But I did have much difficulty in lifting her out. The other smaller dog sprained her paw. I tried getting some advice on how I could close up the pool, but no one had feasible solutions. I started using the pool as my storage area for the merchandise from Casa de Inspiracion. Boxes and boxes of new merchandise and layaways crowded the 33 feet by 12 foot dry pool (area).

The day that had been a premonition by many—someone falling in the open pool and hurting themselves—arrived as predicted.

Several weeks after my auto accident, and after several trips to a chiropractor, while I was frantically trying to get all my paperwork for the tax accountant, I carelessly tripped over a misplaced, open box that lay by the pool. I fell face down. Instead of being concerned about any injures, I was angered by my carelessness. I furiously, threw down the tax papers and stumbled into bed. When I woke up about midnight, I realized that I could be seriously injured and not know it. I cautiously tested and turned my head. I was shocked! Instead of an injury, I had received an adjustment! The neck pain as the consequence of the automobile accident was no longer painful! I could turn my head 180 degrees! How could that have happened?

In the morning, curiously, I retraced my previous night's actions and fall. Surprised, I saw that I had fallen on top of boxes that contained statues of Saint Michael the Archangel! My chin hit one of those boxes and obviously gave me the adjustment that I needed to get rid of a very painful, stiff neck. I don't think that was a coincidence!

Healing Plants and Herbs

Zelima, a Native American from Central America, came into our sphere of knowledge through a Pima College course. A graduate of a Catholic University in California, she decided, after teaching in California awhile, that a better place for her was Tucson, using the herbs of the desert.

Her herbal oils and recipes were incredibly healing. There was one in particular that once I made it and shared it with friends, made me a guru of the healing oil. It is too bad that I lost the recipe. And also lost touch with Zelima. She moved to a monastery somewhere in Texas.

The herbal oils had to be made according to her Native American tradition. Along with drumming, prayer was essential. Communion with nature was important, touching the earth with our bare feet, touching a tree and facing the four winds was a directive. While meditating in prayer, we mixed the numerous oils and herbs to create several bottle of an ointment that healed, according to those with whom I shared it, acne, headaches, bruises, the list was big.

Each of us in the class spent approximately $60.00 on materials. It was very important, Zelima warned us, that we gift this oil with love and prayer. "Never sell or charge anyone for the healing oil."

Here is an example of the power of this oil. During the remodeling of my house, the contractor excused himself, saying, "I must leave. I have a horrendous headache. I just moved to Phoenix, and if I don't take off now, I will never make it. This headache will turn into a migraine. Please, do you have any thing I can take for the pain?" I could think of nothing, except the oil! But I had no idea if this would work on a migraine. I offered it to him.

"Take this oil and massage it on your temples and the back of your head," I said. He did just that and took off. He needed to rush off to make sure he got to his medications before it turned into a migraine.

Several hours later, he called and excitedly told me that his headache was gone several minutes after he left my house. "I was driving by Home Depot," he said, "when I remembered that I had to purchase some drywall." He said that he had completely forgotten his “excruciating” headache! “This type of cure has never happened to me.” He was so excited he wanted to buy some oil from me.

“I can’t sell. But I can give you one of my bottles.” Anyone who received a bottle from me called it Angie’s oil. I called it Zelima’s oil. My father, who shared his oil with friends, called it the magic oil or Raul’s oil.

I personally had no good reason to use the oil. That is, until one day when I suffered two giant bruises, one on each thigh. Figuring this was a good time to test the healing power of this medicated oil, I massaged one thigh with the healing oil and left the other one alone. The one with the oil healed almost immediately; within one day, the bruise began to disappear, while the other one lasted for weeks.

Zelima also appeared to be healer. I made an appointment to have her work on my tendonitis elbow aggravated by playing tennis. Previous visits to doctors and chiropractors had not alleviated the pain.

While she was working on me, she told me that there was something wrong with my head. I advised her that, yes, that was correct. “In approximately ten days, I am scheduled to have a follow-up MRI to check on a brain aneurysm that was previously diagnosed by two different doctors, one in Tucson and another in California. Two angiograms found the aneurism to be the size of a pin, not yet a danger but it required that I exercise certain limitations and be tested every five years.”

She then advised me that she would do away with the affliction. She chanted and prayed over me with an eagle feather for about two hours. Ten days later, I had the MRI. The results surprised me. No aneurism! Were the doctors surprised? No, they stated that the previous diagnosis must have been a mistake.

Zelima never charged me for her service, nor did she ever charge anyone. She said it was a gift from God.

Dominican Priests

My normal routine was to arrive at the store at about 4:30 in the late afternoon in order to relieve Evelyn, my cousin. One such afternoon as I parked my car in front of the store window, I saw six very tall men all dressed in white flowing gown. My first fleeting thought was that there were angels floating around in the store. I walked in and found that they were Dominican priests from San Francisco who had come to Tucson for a seminar. The head priest was Father Anthony. "Saint Anthony, I love that name," I said. "He changed my way of thinking about saints."

He replied that Saint Anthony was his favorite saint, also, and that was the reason he took his name as a priest. "Like everyone else, that saint always helped me find things." Smiling, he said he didn't always like asking him for help because he had promised Saint Anthony that every time he found something he would donate to the Saint Anthony charity a certain percentage of the value of the item found. The most difficult was when he lost a two thousand dollar scholarship check. He had looked everywhere with no success. As the time approached for him to register for college, he became very concerned. He had to give in and ask Saint Anthony for help. He was reluctant. He delayed several more days. Finally, he threw up his hands up in the air. He begged Saint Anthony for help.

He said, "Lo and behold, within minutes, Saint Anthony found the two thousand dollar check!"

I asked him if he donated the 10 percent to charity as he promised. He told me that it hurt to donate that much, but donate he did.

The Poster of the Virgen de Guadalupe When is a miracle considered a miracle? What makes one believe in such incredible events as miracles?

A woman came into the store who had changed and created a glittery picture of the serious image of a poster of the Virgin de Guadalupe. Why did she do this? Her story was interesting.

"I went shopping," she said, "for glitter, paints, makeup, etc. I entered my house, and as I put down my packages on the bed, I heard a soft voice saying, 'Use some of those items to decorate my picture!'." She couldn't figure from where the voice was coming. It repeated the message, and she finally was astonished to realize that it was coming from the picture. She felt she was hearing things and was somewhat frightened. She couldn't figure from where this picture poster had come. Who had put it in her room?

Her husband was not home. She had construction going on in the backyard. She went and asked the workers, "Did any of you put this poster in my room?" No one admitted to doing it. *Besides, who would be so audacious as to enter her house without permission,* she wondered.

The voice had been so sweet and yet so alarmingly urgent that she decided to decorate the picture, even if it was her imagination that heard the voice.

She used sequins, glitter, and makeup to beautifully decorate the poster. It took her days. When she finished, she went and stood it on the kitchen counter.

She started talking and praying to the beautiful image. The next thing that happened took her totally by surprise. She was knocked to the floor as if slain in the spirit. She didn't understand! However, she seemed to hear a voice again that said, "Take me to others so that other people can see who I am."

She took it to a group of her relatives who were praying for a miracle healing. The sick member of the family was healed. The word spread. Before she knew it, many people were requesting to have her take the image to sick people's home. It began to take a toll on her, so instead of presenting it herself at every prayer group that asked, she started lending it out. Some people with afflictions would report that they were healed.

Another thing, the picture would knock on the glass, as if to tell you the Virgin was present.

This matter, the picture and the events, spooked me a bit and made me uncomfortable. But I was curious. The woman volunteered to leave it at the store so that we could introduce it to the many customers who were beginning to ask about the image. We displayed it. Many people came in and prayed before the image. It was beautiful to see.

Some of my Benedictine nun friends wanted to see it. I left it there overnight. To be honest, I was afraid to hear it knock in the middle of the night. I didn't know what I would do if I heard it. The nuns thought it was glittery and very pretty. They didn't hear it knock.

The Church does not recognize miracles until a lengthy process of proving them has been completed. So accepting miracles experienced by the observers of this image was not to be made public in a church setting. However, somehow, it escaped tradition, and Saint Ambrose hosted a service and presentation of the miraculous image. Because the church was packed and the presentation had already started, when a representative from the bishop's office came to stop the event, it was too late.

The last day that the image was in the store, the brother of a very good high school friend of mine came into Casa de Inspiracion. I was showing him the picture and telling him what some people had experienced when they prayed to that image of the Virgin de Guadalupe. (That is, that she knocked on the glass.) I think I half believed it. But she knocked as I spoke. I can't explain how I felt, but it shocked me. It actually brought tears to my eyes. I was startled and worked hard to keep back the tears.

The woman who created the image moved to California. We never heard from her again.

Saint Therese the Little Flower

Saint Therese of Lisieux is not only one of the few female doctors of the Church but she is considered very miraculous. She is one of the most popular saints among the Catholic people. "When I die, I will send down a shower of roses from the heavens. I will spent my time in heaven by doing good on earth," she said before she died. And she does do just that.

There are many books written about her life. Among all the books that we had at the store, there was one in particular that had a lifelike photograph of her on the cover. I decided that that was the one I wanted to read. I brought it home. My little dogs greeted me at the door. I fed them right away and then decided to sit down and read. Buffy was the more sensitive of the two dogs. When Buffy saw the picture of Saint Therese the Little Flower, on the cover, he started barking at it and wagging his tail as if he were seeing a real person. He wouldn't stop. He was excited. I was startled and a little spooked. "What was he seeing?" I asked myself.

I tried to make him stop. "Buffy, stop barking!" He wouldn't, so I put the book away where he could not see the photograph. The next day, again, I brought down the book with the photograph of Saint Therese the Little Flower. Again, Buffy greeted her with a bark and the wag of his tail. I will never know what he was sensing, but Buffy was a very special, sensitive dog. When his fifteen-year-old brother was dying, he cried and howled and tried to force him to get up. I had to remove Buffy from the room. His sadness was overwhelming.

The Unexplained Apparition of the Virgin Mary in the Bell Tower

"I saw an apparition of the Virgin Mary!" A young lady had excitedly shared this incredible experience with us as she came into the Casa de Inspiracion.

In the small town of Eloy, the Virgin was appearing in the bell tower of a Catholic church. It was played down by the priest. But evidently, it became popular knowledge after a group of people saw it as they walked out of the church. They had just finished a Cursillo gathering. It was late evening. We understand it was the deacon who first saw it. He fell to his knees in prayer, and the other cursillistas followed suit.

At first big groups of people were meeting after sunset to see the apparition, to pray, and to be blessed by the vision. The priest there claimed that it could be a reflection of some kind. He climbed up into the tower and had it painted, hoping to diffuse whatever light was creating this excitement. But there was no getting rid of the image that appeared almost every evening after dusk. To make certain that it was not some kind of optical illusion, a Spanish TV station came with their brightest of bright lights and focused them on the image in the bell tower. They could not make it disappear.

I don't know how popular these events were outside of Eloy. We heard about it because a young businesswoman came to the store and claimed she would smell roses every time she drove by Eloy. She had decided to investigate the source and was told that it was symbolic of the presence of the Virgin Mary. "If that is so, where is the Virgin Mary?" she asked.

A gas station attendant told her, "She appears at the Catholic church across from the high school." When the young woman told us she saw the apparition in the bell tower of the church, we, myself and two other friends, decided to investigate it for ourselves. We left Tucson and arrived late in spite of several mishaps that seemed determined to prevent our getting there.

A small group was praying the rosary when we got to the church. And sure enough, we saw a translucent figure, like Lalique glass, up in the tower. It definitely resembled the Virgin Mary. She was holding the Baby Jesus. All three of us saw the same thing. (I say this because we decided to go home and sketch out what we each had seen, either to verify the image or to prove that our minds were playing a trick on us. We each drew the same image.)

Several years later, my husband and I were driving back from Phoenix and passing through Eloy. I told him about my experience there. He was skeptical and said he would have to see it for himself. It wasn't much later that he asked to go to Eloy, to Saint Helen's Church, where a relic of the true cross upon which Christ was crucified is exposed. We got there just as they were closing the church, but he was able to get some information from the secretary that verified my story about the visions. Now he was more interested and wanted to make sure that he was present at the supposed time that she appeared. We went to dinner, and we were back at the church just in time for the sun to set. We waited ten or so minutes for dusk. Unexpectedly, there was a black and white image in the bell tower standing next to the church bell. It appeared to be a veiled woman holding a book. Goose bumps and unexpected tears filled our eyes. We prayed the rosary and remained there silently for some time.

On the way home, we called our priest. He verified that we were considered very blessed, for not everyone who went there got the opportunity to see her apparition.

My husband decided he wanted to do research and write about these apparitions. He learned that the church claims it to be a natural phenomenon but couldn't get an exact answer as to what that meant. He was given permission from the church to interview the people who volunteered to share their experiences. They all claimed it was definitely an apparition of the Virgin Mary. Some had miraculous healings for themselves, relatives, or friends for which they petitioned. Several said that they stood there with a skeptical friend or relative who saw nothing while they themselves saw the Virgin Mary.

The Infant of Prague

One day, a woman and her niece walked into the store. The younger woman startled me as she quickly looked around and yelled in surprise, "That is the image! That is the statue we want!" It was a beautiful statue of the Infant of Prague, dressed in a red velvet cape.

As I took it down from the shelf, she told me how miraculous the Infant of Prague novena had been in their lives. (Novenas are a series of prayers said for nine consecutive days.) Apparently, while playing golf, her eleven-year-old son had been struck by lightning. The doctors did not expect him to survive, or if he did live, he would be seriously handicapped. He had been placed on three life support systems.

Her aunt told the family not to give in to the horrible prognosis. "God is powerful. Let's start a novena to the Infant of Prague. The Infant of Prague is very miraculous," she said. And sure enough, on the ninth day as they ended the novena, one of the attending physician called the house. He had wonderful news. "Your son can have one of the three life support machines removed." That wasn't all!

On the second and third day each after this news, the doctors announced they could remove the son off the other two life support machines. This was a boy whom the doctors had not expected to live. They were shocked and could not believe he had made such a miraculous recovery.

The family returned to the site where their son had been struck by lightning. They wanted to offer more prayers in gratitude for the miracle. To their surprise, they found, on a rock, the little cross that their son had been wearing when he was struck. They will be forever grateful that this young boy not only survived but in the end, suffered absolutely no ill effects from the accident.

Because of this incident, the next advertisement that we placed in *The Vision*, a diocese Catholic newspaper, included a photograph of the Infant of Prague. Surprisingly, that photograph attracted a lot of attention and brought us many new customers. Many, many statues of the Infant of Prague were eventually sold. We could not keep them in stock. I had had no idea He was so popular.

Alex Suffers the Stigmata

One day, Olga invited me to a lecture by Alex, a relatively young man of about twenty-nine who was suffering the stigmata. His journey was very interesting.

As a child, Alex loved praying before the crucifix. When he grew into his teenage years, he said he would spent hours in front of the Holy Eucharist and the crucifix. One day, however, Mormons moved into his neighborhood. He ended up falling in love with a young Mormon girl, marrying her, and converting to her religion. Eventually, they moved to Utah.

However, he realized that things had changed too fast for him. He began to search for his old faith, secretly attending Catholic services when he could sneak away. Eventually, he informed his wife that he needed to return to Catholicism. The elders could not accept this, and they encouraged a divorce.

Then one day, he had an apparition. A beautiful lady, the Virgin Mary, appeared and had a favor to ask of him. "Would you be willing to suffer the stigmata?"

"Why me? Why do you want me to suffer the stigmata?" She appeared three times, each time encouraging him and begging that he sacrifice and show the world his faith in the crucifix and Christ. He consented.

He covered his wounds, the hands and feet, with bandages, thus covering the bleeding wounds of the stigmata. A strong smell of roses emanated from this body. Each time that I saw him (I saw him three of the numerous times he came to Tucson), the cross on his forehead became deeper and deeper. The last visit I attended was a question and answer session. I asked if he suffered the trials that Padre Pio had suffered, the attacks by the demon, the devil. Without much detail, He simply answered yes. But Olga later attested to the fact that he would end up at the hospital with broken bones and such, as he was often attacked and thrown around in his bedroom in the middle of the night.

Alex suffered many setbacks. He endured suffering in many ways. He did what the Virgin Mary asked of him, but it was not an easy journey. The Church itself did not make it easy for him. Understandably, because of church law, a bishop cannot take under his wing a person seeing or experiencing visions. For example, he was scheduled to speak at the Benedictine monastery but at the last minute was told he could not give a talk in the church nor could he show his wounds. (The Church does this to protect itself from many false claims. The Church is obligated to first verify that these signs are truly from God.)

The last time I saw Alex was before I had a big fall in my house. Before we were scheduled to go see Alex, Lydia and I rushed home to feed my dogs. I walked into the kitchen, the handle of a dust broom became entangled in my feet, as if lanced, and I fell. I never figured out how that happened. Although I slipped all across the kitchen floor, I was unhurt. I got back into the car and told Lydia what had happened. We both laughed because that was my seventh weird and unexplained fall during that year. We listened to Alex and when he was through with his lecture, we went up for a blessing. As I approached him, I could smell roses, that incredible sign that the Virgin Mary is present. I told him about my many falls at Lourdes, at the Washington Memorial in Washington, D.C., at the Benjamin Franklin Museum, and so on. It was just one fall after another.

Alex said, "It sounds like an evil force, the Devil, is trying to keep you from doing something. What is it that you do?" I replied that I had a religious store. He asked that I pray to Saint Michael and my guardian angel for protection. Sure enough, I prayed to both and never suffered another fall.

Alex died shortly after. He had been thrown up against the wall and had been very badly injured. He died from several of those beating. He died young.

Sister Carmela

I was fortunate to meet Sister Carmela, the Benedictine icon artist from the monastery here in Tucson. Her icons were a wonderful addition to the inventory in the store. We became good friends. Whenever possible we went out to dinner and even took several trips together with other friends.

I was curious what encouraged her to become a nun.

She said she was a slightly mischievous youngster—religiously mischievous, that is. In her small town, she would participate in running a booth for her church during an annual pilgrimage when a large number of very faithful people would come from all over. They numbered in the thousands. Every year, she and her friends who worked at the booth remarked to each other how weird these people seemed, carrying icons, praying the rosary, and so on. This attitude continued for a number of years until she approached the age of sixteen and had an epiphany. Then when she turned seventeen, she advised her mother that she desired to become a nun. Her mother had already enrolled her in a nursing college. She said there was no turning back.

However, Sister Carmela had a different idea. She was determined to become a nun. She prayed to Saint Therese the Little Flower. "Send me a message. Verify that I need to follow my calling to become a nun." She asked Saint Therese to send a dozen roses. "To be certain that you are talking to me, let the roses be yellow on the inside and pink on the outside." An order that was nearly impossible to fulfill unless it truly came from heaven.

The very next day, one of the nursing students knocked on her dorm door. She asked Sister Carmela if she wanted the bouquet of a dozen roses that she held in her hands. "This bouquet was left at the door. No one knows where it came from. It was just left there."

The roses were yellow on the inside and pink on the outside, just as she had prayed for. By this time, Sister Carmela had been communicating with the nuns at the convent where she wanted to be. She immediately packed her bags and left for the convent. When she arrived, she called her mother. She advised her that she was already at the convent and was ready to follow her dream to become a nun.

Surprisingly, several weeks after she had related this story to me, she called. She asked me if I had sent her a dozen roses, yellow on the inside and pink on the outside. She hardly believed me when I stuck to my story. I truly had not sent those roses. "They were left at the door of the monastery, and one of the nuns handed them to me as I walked down the hall. You are the only person who knew about this!" she said.

We both believe that Saint Therese the Little Flower, again, sent them to reaffirm her calling.

ST. BENEDICT
Sr. Carmela

ST. FRANCIS
Sr. Carmela

Cross of Holy Father Benedict
May the Holy Cross be my Light.
May the dragon be not my leader:
Be gone Satan!
not with deceits.
offered is evil.
poison yourself.
PEACE
PAX
Sr. Carmela

Sr. Carmela

ST. MICHAEL

The Helpful Young Boy Who Later Became a Priest

Tony, who was just a child at the time, would come to a convent located in the Midwest. He would carry his guitar in order to sing and volunteer to work for the nuns.

He was an active and extroverted youngster, probably about seven. He would volunteer to do chores, like mopping the floors or whatever else the nuns needed. After the chores were completed, he would sing for the nuns, "whether or not we wanted him to sing," Sister Carmela said and laughed as she told me about Tony.

Tony was of Italian descent, was very tall, and grew to be a vigorous, outgoing man. Still young, he entered the seminary and ended up becoming a parish priest in a small mountain village in Peru. He loved working with the Peruvian villagers and decided that with their help, they would build a cathedral. He was enthusiastic and full of ideas. Little did he know that a small village far away from a major city did not qualify for a cathedral. Nor did he know that he needed the approval of the bishop.

When the bishop came to the village, he said to Father Tony, "You must have the permission of the bishop to build a cathedral; I'm the bishop, and I'm not giving you permission. Not in a small village like this." Either Father Tony thought that the bishop was kidding or he decided he was too far along to stop. He continued working with the villagers.

Father Tony enjoyed the delight and enthusiasm of the indigenous people. They worked hard. But a troubling problem developed. When they were about to finish, Father Tony realized that he did not have the necessary funds to pay for the roof. He worried. He did not know where or from whom he would get the money. He went into the church and began to talk to Saint Therese the Little Flower. He prayed aloud. "I need two thousand dollars. And I need it tomorrow." As he was praying, someone tapped him on the shoulder. He signaled with the back of his hand that he could not talk. He was busy talking to Saint Therese. The person, whoever it was, handed him a piece of paper. He accepted it and, a bit distracted, placed it into his pocket. He continued praying and thought no more about the paper.

Later that evening as he walked to his room, he remembered the note in his pocket. He became dismayed at the thought that, perhaps, someone had been in dire need of a priest. Concerned, he quickly retrieved the paper. He stared at what looked like a cashier's check. To his surprise, it was for two thousand dollars! *Two thousand dollars!* No one knew he need that exact amount. No one except Saint Therese the Little Flower!

"No one will convince me that it wasn't Saint Therese," he said as he shared some of the ways this saint had helped him all his life, since he was a child. Father Tony died at a young age while traveling by bus from Lima back to his village up in the mountains. He suffered a heart attack and, I do believe, he went to heaven.

Michael the Warlock

This story frightens me somewhat. One who doesn't believe in witches might change their mind after hearing this story.

One day, a man by the name of Michael came into the store. He became a frequent customer. He loved visiting the store and would mention how beautiful the items were and how he couldn't get enough of them. "Do you wonder why I purchase so many of these items?" he asked but didn't wait for my response. He told me that he had been a warlock, a man who practiced witchcraft, a sorcerer. He had achieved a very high position as a warlock and that at his level, one couldn't just leave the coven of those with whom he had bonded. The other warlocks would kill him if they located him. He shared that their evil powers were very strong, and the only things that kept him safe were the scapular, rosaries, and prayers. Sacred pictures, also, were very powerful tools against the evil forces of the witches. He said, "People have no idea how much protection there is in prayers, sacred items, and the Church."

It was his intention to join the Knights of Columbus, and he did. He desired to do missionary work in the neighborhood, and he required the protection of sacramentals to keep him from harm. He was adamant that witches and warlocks were very powerful.

Father Bliven

Father Bliven was an extremely interesting priest with lots of beautiful spiritual powers about which I do not feel at liberty to speak, but I do want to share a miracle that he believed saved his life.

He was transferred to Hermosillo, Mexico, from Ramona, California, because in Ramona, his life was threatened by gang members. Apparently, he was doing missionary work on the side to convert young gang members who were meeting in the park. He was convincing them to go to church, to attend Mass, and to go to confess. Fearing that he knew too much, leaders of the gangs put a contract out for his death.

In Hermosillo, he built shelters for the homeless, the drug addicts, the unwed mothers, and the poor. There was sometimes danger in what he did, and by his own admission, he was "getting somewhat cocky" and believed that because he was helping so many, nothing bad would ever happen to him.

However, one night around midnight, there was a knock on his door. He was confronted by a drug addict who overpowered him, tied him up with wires, and said, "After you watch me take everything of value out of your house, you are going to die." He propped open the door and started taking out the television, the computer, and so on from the house and putting them right into a truck.

Father Bliven started a prayer chain to Saint Michael the Archangel, defender against evil. Just as the intruder was about finished and took out one of the last loads, the door slammed shut, locking itself. As a result, the thief could not reenter. Father Bliven's life was saved. He strongly advised me that it was his sincere belief that Saint Michael the Archangel had knocked the prop loose and slammed and locked the door, thus leaving the thief out in the cold.

Bad things happen to good people.

Father Bliven got pneumonia going out in a storm to try to get funds for a very sick patient who was being denied admittance to the hospital in Hermosillo because she did not have the means to pay. He drove all the way from Hermosillo to Douglas to get the money from a Tucson donor. It was very cold, and he was very tired. From the exposure to the extreme cold, he got pneumonia and died. The newspapers reported that his funeral was held outside the church because there was no room inside to hold the hundreds and hundreds of people who attended his service. They said the flowers in front of the church were comparable to those showered for Princess Diana.

A Deacon's Story

One day, a deacon received a long distance call on his cell phone. A gentleman, a stranger by the name of Joseph proceeded to inform the deacon that he was responsible for Joseph and his family's plans to leave their denomination and become Catholics. The deacon was baffled and said, "Back up a little bit and explain to me what is happening. I don't believe I know you." The caller told him that he had seen him on Facebook in a healing ministry. He not only liked what the deacon had said about the Eucharist, Jesus, and Padre Pio but he believed that through the deacon, God was sending him a message. He was determined to move a long distance from northern California to Tucson to learn about the Catholic Church from the deacon.

"God was telling me to convert to Catholicism through you. Therefore, I plead with you, Deacon, that since you are responsible for this conversion and move in my life, to pray for me, my family, and a group of followers that are coming with me. This move will have a regional effect on my church, the Assembly of God."

"I am at your service. Anything I can do to help you, I will do," the deacon responded. They made plans to meet at the Tucson church where the deacon was a senior deacon when Joseph, his wife, and his followers arrived.

About two months after their first and only conversation, Joseph, his wife, and quite a few other people arrived in Tucson. They truly were settling in Tucson. They needed to find jobs and asked if the deacon would help. Besides, Joseph was sure God would provide everything for them. The deacon referred him to the priest, who was in the position of helping converts. Also, the deacon reassured Joseph that he would be there to help in any way that he could.

The meeting with the priest was set up. They underwent a period of Catholic instruction for about six months. They were serious about taking advantage of several different ministries and learning everything they needed to know.

One Wednesday when the Blessed Sacrament was to be exposed for adoration, events started to become obvious to the deacon about his required involvement in their conversion. The group announced that they would be present for adoration. The deacon explained, "We, being people of faith, believe in the real presence of Jesus in the Blessed Sacrament and also that the kingdom of God is present with Jesus. We take this very seriously."

The deacon situated the Blessed Sacrament on the altar and made all necessary preparations for adoration. As he sat down to catch his breath, he received a message, a word of wisdom from God. "I want my son and daughter (Joseph and his wife) to come up before me in front of the Blessed Sacrament. I am going to bless them as my children, as my disciples, as my followers, and as my son and daughter. You, Deacon, will initiate that because you are responsible for them, in praying throughout life for them."

The deacon felt the huge load he had taken on. "Is this reality, or am I dreaming?" he asked himself. "No, this is reality. I will go up to where they are seated, lead them up to the Holy Eucharist, and position them before the Blessed Sacrament." The deacon did as exactly as told. He brought them before the Blessed Sacrament. They were crying and weeping strongly, like babies. They knew that God was calling them through the deacon, Padre Pio, and the blessed Mother of God. The presence of the Blessed Sacrament had doubled the effect on them as much as it had on the deacon. He prayed for them; the entire community present in the church prayed for them for about five to ten minutes as they continued crying.

The experience was incredible and unusual for all. They were glad that they found God. They found the calling.

Joseph stayed with the priest and his church for about a month. After receiving the sacraments, they went to a small neighboring town near Tucson where they settled. There Joseph became the director of the town's youth ministry. Under his direction, the membership of the youth ministry multiplied three or four times in number.

Often, now, the deacon visits with Joseph and his followers whenever they all have a chance.

A GIFT OF LOVE

The Power of the Rosary

Father Showri completed his summer ministry as a seminarian at one of the shrines in India. His responsibilities were numerous. Besides taking care of the church campus, the pilgrims, the tourists, and the visitors, he had to care for the water buffaloes: clean and wash them and their bedding.

"Also, at night someone had to keep watch of the shrine campus. The parish priest, also named Father Showri—a popular name in India, meaning Xavier, since Saint Xavier is buried in India—asked if I would do so, meaning I would sleep outside," Father Showri said.

The church property was very large and entirely enclosed by a wall. The rectory was in one corner, and the shrine was in the middle of the campus. Also in the middle was the structure where the buffalo be would tied up at night.

"Before any structures were built, a Hindu family donated the entire land to the church. The ancestral tombs were there on the property. The fact that there were tombs on the property did not bother me at all. The presence of any cemetery has never disturbed me, even as a youth.

"Every night before I went to sleep, I had to carry out to the campus a large blanket and a narrow bed just wide enough to accommodate my body comfortably. As usual, I would place my rosary next to the side of my head. I would pray before I went to sleep. A habit I learned from my grandmother.

"One night, exhausted, I fell asleep before I finished praying. I was forcibly awakened during the middle of the night. There was an incredible weight pressing down on my chest, making it very difficult to breathe. I tried to open my eyes, but I could not. I tried to speak, but I could not. I attempted to reach for my rosary that always lay beside me, but it was not there. My rosary had slipped off the bench and was on the ground! I struggled violently against something that felt very evil.

"Finally, after a long violent struggle, I was able to reach down to the ground and touch the rosary with my hand. Immediately, this evil force let go and disappeared. When I recovered, I realized that I was soaking wet from perspiration. This included my undershirt, my shirt, and my pants. I sat up and drank some water, finished praying the rosary, and was able to fall back to sleep.

"When I shared this event with my pastor, he replied that yes, he was aware of two or three demons who were on the property. Up until then, he hadn't mentioned them. When asked why he hadn't mentioned these demons before, he said, 'Who would want to sleep outside if they knew about the two or three demons!'

"It didn't bother me. I had no further encounters. I continued to sleep outside every night until I finished summer ministry at the shrine with the rosary secure around my neck! I made sure to wear the rosary. That prevented it from falling were I to fall asleep while praying. Since that time, for protection, I always wear the Our Lady, Undoer of Knots rosary around my neck."

Angels Protected Father Showri as a Baby This story is from Father Showri's point of view.

I was born at home in my Grandmother's house in the1970s. In those days, my family had a farm with water buffaloes. We had no water facilities so we had to walk a good distance, four blocks, to draw our daily water supply from a common well. We would pour it into metal vases (*bindelu* in Telugu) and would bring the vases back to the house, where we would then empty them into a common reservoir. This would take several trips before the reservoir was filled. We used this water not only for all of our family's needs, like drinking, cooking, and bathing, but also to water the buffaloes.

Customarily, when the women went to get the water, the men of the family would go into the fields and, with a scythe, cut several bundles of grass to feed the buffaloes. They would place these bundles in that part of the walled compound where the buffaloes would stay and feed.

It happened one day when I was just five days old. The women left me in a cradle in the yard while they went to get the water. After they left for what was to be the last trek, my uncle came with several bundles of grass all tied up and laid them just beyond where I lay in my crib. Shortly after, the buffaloes began to return home. They entered the walled compound. Smelling and seeing the bundles of grass just beyond my crib, they walked around me. Anxious and hungry, they began to tug and fight each other for the feed. They were all around me. They collapsed the cradle, which was made of dried and tied grass, on which my crib rested. The crib and I fell to the ground.

By this time, my mother, grandmother, and aunt approached the walled compound with the water jugs and saw the buffaloes fighting and milling around the area where they had left me. No one could see me but could see the pieces of the collapsed and strewn grass cradle. My mother, overcome with fear, fell to the ground, certain that I had been trampled to death.

I was not only the oldest boy in the family, I was the only boy on both sides of the family, a position considered very precious to all of my mother's and father's relatives. It was traditionally expected that I take over my father's role when he was no longer able to care for the family. Now, totally distraught, my mother and my aunt believed I was gone.

My aunt walked away from the others to go to fetch my body but discovered that I was laying there between the buffaloes' legs, untouched and unharmed. I appeared to be playing, not even crying. My aunt picked me up and took me to my other, who was exhilarated beyond belief. The buffaloes, however, continued fighting and milling around.

To this day, they still can't bear to think about the potential consequences of that fateful day, definitely a miracle in their eyes. My mother later told me that the reason the angels protected me was due to my grandmother's wonderful custom of blessing the corners of each bed with the sign of the cross whenever she left the house. I, too, definitely believe the angels protected me because of my grandmother's blessing.

Rosaries Are of Extreme Importance to Father Showri

Often while on the plane, flying from airport to airport, I pray the rosary as a part of everyday meal. One of these times, the rosary that I carried in my pocket, unbeknownst to me, fell—"surely between the two seats," I later figured out.

When we landed in Dallas, Texas, we were rushed out of the aircraft. I had to connect with another flight. All of a sudden, I realized I didn't have my rosary! I then knew that it fell while back in the airplane from which I had just exited. I returned and tried to enter the aircraft but was stopped by airline personnel. I explained to them that I had lost my rosary and was certain it remained under the seat where I had been sitting. They replied that they had not come across any rosary while they were cleaning and preparing the aircraft for its next flight. They adamantly explained that I could not go back in because they had completed preparing it for the next flight. I became persistent. I, too, was adamant and advised them that the rosary was very precious and I was not going to leave until I got it back. I would remain right where I was and would miss my next connection if necessary. They finally relented and told me they would go back into the aircraft to look for it. I insisted on going in with them. When I got to my seat, I reached down and found it!

I lost it again at the same airport but this time, not in an aircraft. Somehow, it slipped out of the pocket bag. When I called Lost and Found to ask them if anyone had turned in a rosary, they replied that they had not yet received one but when they did, they would mail it to me, and they took the mailing address. A month later, they mailed the rosary to me. Allow me to list some reasons why this rosary is so important to me and I was persistent to get it back.

1. This particular rosary is made with the olive wood from Bethlehem and has a copper chain.
2. This rosary has traveled around the globe many times.
3. This rosary was blessed by touching the tombs of the twenty saints (First Class Relics), such as Mother Teresa, Saint Thomas the Apostle, Saint Francis Xavier, and so on.

4. This rosary has been twice placed in the tomb of Jesus in Jerusalem and placed on the original holy cross of Jesus and been blessed.
5. Almost three holy Fathers (Popes), including Saint Pope John Paul II, blessed this rosary. It has been blessed three time by Pope Francis.

"Many people have asked me for this rosary," Father said, "but sincerely, I always reply, 'Sorry, no!'."

Prayers and Miracles

"This event is very vivid in my mind because it just happened," Father Showri said as we interviewed him, asking him about miracles that he had experienced in his occupation.

"I completed my Divine Mercy Chaplet a little after three o'clock in the afternoon. I was between Masses at Saint Mary's Hospital and Saint Joseph's Hospital and was preparing to go celebrate the five o'clock mass at Saint Francis de Sales Parish. My first thought, however, was to finish making the rounds in the hospitals' ICUs. It was then that I was approached by a nurse. She asked if I would bless a young man of thirty-three years of age who was dying.

"As I walked into the patient's room, it was easy to notice that the family was very sad. I went to his bed. His father, mother, and sister were there. They sobbed.

"When they first saw me, they didn't realize I was a priest. I told them I was a Catholic priest. But they seemed unsure. They looked at my long hair and beard. I informed them that I was a hospital chaplain and I was there to bless their son. They did not react to my words. The young adult was intubated and unconscious. They believed that he would soon pass, probably within the next day. When I repeated that I was there to give him a blessing, the sister cried and said, 'Please do.'

"'I am going to give him an anointing, if you are alright with that.' I told them.

"'Please, please anoint him.' The sister responded.

"We prayed the prayer of the anointing of the sick together. I anointed him on the forehead, both his hands, and both his legs. I gave communion to both parents and the sister. Suddenly, there was a stir. The young patient started shaking his left hand. This continued for a few minutes. His sister jumped with joy. She exclaimed, 'He's moving! He's shaking his hand!'

"He was also saying his name. He opened his eyes. The entire family reacted with real joy. He was alive. The mother cried out, 'It's a miracle!'

"I told them that I would offer the next mass for him. Then we prayed for him.

“The nurses came in. They, too, were surprised. They had not believed that he could respond. The fact that he responded meant he was getting better. That was a miracle. We then all prayed the Our Father together.

“Many miracles happen with the power of prayer.

“Today, he is doing well. He appears to have recovered. When one of the nurses asked me about the miracle I performed, I reminded her that was not me but God through prayer who performed the miracle.”

A Miracle of the Scapular

I called Father Showri. "I think Richard may now need the last rites. You recently administered a healing ritual. Was that considered a last rite? If not, since you are still out of town, should I call Father Bala?"

"Yes," Father Showri replied. "Have Father Bala come and administer the last rites. Or you can wait until Thursday when I will return, if you believe there is time."

I decided to wait. It was only a day-and-a-half wait. In the meantime, I felt that I needed to take Richard a scapular, a picture of the Divine Mercy, and holy water (not ordinary holy water but of that blessed and used in exorcism).

I also took a battery-powered candle and a cloth with a beautiful picture of the Virgin de Guadalupe.

When I arrived, I was happy to see Richard's cousin, Brenda, sitting there. Richard was very agitated, moaning and tossing in pain. His breathing was very labored and rough. I explained to Brenda what I had brought and how important these items were in these anticipated last moments.

With a little bit of difficulty, we hung up the framed picture of the Divine Mercy. I blessed Richard with the holy water, making the sign of the cross on his forehead and sprinkling it over him and his bed.

I asked Brenda if she remembered the meaning of the scapular. "Very vaguely," she replied.

"The Virgin Mary has promised that anyone wearing the scapular when they die are assured to go to heaven." I held up his head, and we slipped the scapular around his neck. Richard's unexpected reaction was a total surprise to both of us. His extremely agitated body and labored breathing suddenly became peaceful and serene. We looked at one another incredulously, as if we had truly seen a miracle.

We spoke softly and reverently, both breathless by the event we had just witnessed. She claimed that as a child making her First Communion, she had been taught about the miracles of the scapular but had forgotten them as she grew into adulthood.

After she left, I recited the Divine Mercy Chaplet and the rosary. Richard was more familiar with the rosary than the Divine Mercy, and I desired that even though he was not conscious, he would be able to hear the prayers as we have been taught that hearing is the last faculty that leaves.

Before I departed, I moistened his mouth with a straw. Richard was very peaceful.

The following morning, his brother, Jeffry, called to give me the sad news. "Richard passed away at six this morning. I visited him last night," he said. "We had not seen him this peaceful since he entered the hospice here at Villa Maria."

I arrived at Villa Maria just in time. I wanted to make sure to bless his body with holy water before they took him away. It was comforting to see the peaceful look on his face. I made the sign of the cross on his forehead with holy water as the attendants covered his body and took him away.

His soul and spirit are surely with God. I feel that Richard was forgiven for all his sins. His purgatory was here on earth. One morning as I was taking him to a doctor's appointment, he complained that he could not understand why he was suffering so much but if it meant that he was been cleansed of his sins and heaven would be his final destination, he would tolerate it gladly.

He did suffer greatly during his last months on earth.

God bless you, Richard.

ST. MICHAEL